Table of Contents

Rourke
Educational Media
rourkeeducationalmedia.com

A Division of
Carson
Dellosa
Education

Can you find these words?

ears

golden

puppies

sit

Golden Retriever Puppies

puppies

These are Golden Retriever **puppies!**

What do Golden Retriever puppies look like?

They have long **ears**.

They have **golden** fur.

golden

They get big. They grow to 23 inches (58 centimeters) tall.

What do Golden Retriever puppies act like? They like walks.

sit

They can learn to **sit**.

They like to run and play.

This puppy can fetch a ball.

Did you find these words?

They have long **ears**.

They have **golden** fur.

These are Golden Retriever **puppies**!

They can learn to **sit**.

Photo Glossary

 **ears** (eerz): The organs you hear with on either side of the head.

 **golden** (GOHL-duhn): A deep yellow color.

 **puppies** (PUHP-eez): Dogs that are young and not fully grown.

 **sit** (sit): To rest your weight on your hindquarters.

Index

About the Author

Hailey Scragg is a writer from Ohio. She loves all puppies, especially her puppy, Abe! She likes taking him on long walks in the park.

www.rourkeeducationalmedia.com

PHOTO CREDITS: cover: ©Dixi_, ©manley099 (bone); back cover: ©Naddiya (pattern); back cover (inset), page 8: ©chayathonwong; pages 2, 3, 9, 14, 15: ©Bigandt_Photography; pages 2, 4-5, 14, 15: ©Paige_Rigoglioso; pages 2, 6-7, 14, 15: ©StudioByTheSea; page 10: ©skynesher; pages 2, 11, 14, 15: ©MarkoNOVKOV; pages 12-13: ©HollyAA

Edited by: Kim Thompson
Cover and interior design by: Janine Fisher

Library of Congress PCN Data
Golden Retriever Puppies / Hailey Scragg
(Top Puppies)
ISBN 978-1-73162-855-8 (hard cover)(alk. paper)
ISBN 978-1-73162-854-1 (soft cover)
ISBN 978-1-73162-857-2 (e-Book)
ISBN 978-1-73163-338-5 (ePub)
Library of Congress Control Number: 2019945499

Printed in the United States of America,
North Mankato, Minnesota

Book Ends for the Reader

I know...

1. What do Golden Retriever puppies look like?

2. How tall do Golden Retrievers get?

3. What do Golden Retriever puppies act like?

I think...

1. Can Golden Retriever puppies be trained?

2. Do Golden Retriever puppies like people?

3. Do Golden Retriever puppies need exercise?

Golden Retriever Puppies

Golden Retrievers are cute puppies. Find out what Golden Retriever puppies look like, act like, and what makes the Golden Retriever a top puppy!

Books in the series *Top Puppies* include:

Boxer Puppies

Bulldog Puppies

German Shepherd Puppies

Golden Retriever Puppies

Labrador Retriever Puppies

Poodle Puppies

Pug Puppies

Yorkshire Terrier Puppies

Rourke
Educational Media

A Division of
Carson Dellosa Education

rourkeeducationalmedia.com

TARGET SKILLS

Guided Reading Level: **F**

- Develop decoding skills.
- Recognize frequently used words.
- Use text to confirm pronunciation and meaning.
- Make personal connections to a text.

ISBN: 978-1-73162-854-1

9 781731 628541